Pirene's Fountain

Pirene's Fountain
Bridging Divides

Volume 13, Issue 21

Pirene's Fountain: A Journal of Poetry
Volume 13, Issue 21
Copyright © 2020 Pirene's Fountain
Paperback ISSN 2331-1096

Editor: Megan Merchant
Layout, Book & Cover Design: Steven Asmussen
Copyediting: Elizabeth Nichols & Linda E. Kim
Cover Artist: © Martin Lehmann | Dreamstime.com

All rights reserved: except for the purpose of quoting brief passages for review, no part of this book may be reproduced or transmitted in any form or by any means, electronic or mechanical, including photocopying, recording, or by any information storage and retrieval system, without permission in writing from the publisher.

Glass Lyre Press, LLC
P.O. Box 2693
Glenview, IL 60025

www.GlassLyrePress.com

Contents

Poetry

Katie Chicquette Adams
    When You Say the Other 49 Should Copy Alabama   9
Diana Anhalt
    Tierra   10
Amy Baskin
    Back When We Were Dirt   11
Lauren Camp
    Nimble Flies   12
    Large Contrast Examples   13
    Sorry City Sweetly   14
    Here the Awful Happens Elsewhere   16
Sarah Carleton
    English Lessons   17
    The Guardians   18
    Miami Airport Nocturne   19
Patrice Claeys
    Suzanne   20
Roger Craik
    Park of Human Rights, Izmir   22
Sara Comito
    Ghosts on the Center Line   24
    Company Town   25
Darren Demaree
    Emily as the Bird Falls   26
Anuja Ghimire
    cigarette bruise   27
    city girl goes caroling in the village   28
Patrick Hansel
    Mourning in America   29
    A Day Without Immigrants   30
    The Midfielder Bows Down for Prayer   32
Jennifer Jean
    The "John School"   34

Allison Joseph
    Ode to Fast Willie and Friends   36
    Too Many Houses   38

Jennifer Schomburg Kanke
    Summer Sonnet in Orange   39
    The Mullet   40
    To My Neighbor, Coughing Across the Street   41

Lynne Knight
    As If   42
    The Tattoo   43

Rustin Larson
    Northern Vermont   44
    The Tunnel of Snakes   45

Gisèle Lewis
    Sewing lesson   46
    Halloween, 2016   47

Marjorie Maddox
    The Billboard   48

Charissa Menefee
    Tiny Portraits of Men   49

Cameron Morse
    Orchid Garden Residence Community   50
    Offerings   52
    The Names of Children   53

Bruce Pemberton
    Coyote Oblivion   54
    Iraq, September 2004   55

Claudia Reder
    To Nelly Sachs   57

Amy Small-McKinney
    For A Day I Stop Talking   58

Alison Stone
    July 2018   59

Barrett Warner
    Living in the "Birthplace of the Neutrino"   60

Reviews

If the House by Molly Spencer   65
Tunsiya / Amrikiya by Leila Chatti   69
The Number 5 Is Always Suspect by Bob Heman & Cindy Hochman   73

Prompts

Contributor Notes

POETRY

When You Say the Other 49 Should Copy Alabama

Katie Chicquette Adams

I hear "high risk likely"
      fall like tiny unspent bullets
      from my doctor's lips

I hear the number 50,000—
      the number of circulating platelets at which hemorrhage
      occurs from "minor trauma,"
      at which you can't wake up from anesthesia, a number
      once dictated by a malfunctioning placenta
      and by probably every placenta I would ever grow

I hear my bitter laugh, when I admit that contraception
      is a chivalrous knight: trustworthy but fallible

I hear the dull choke of anguish, knowing that I would
      have to let go of a brand new person
      carved from my own heart
      whom I will never know because doing so
      could lead to our deaths

I hear voices I will never meet saying
      I care less about you, an existing person,
      than a series of cells who have not yet bonded
      emotionally to anyone
          the way I have, the way I grow like a vine
          around my children, the way they climb
          me like a scaffold

I hear the ventilator wheeze
I hear the machines beep
I hear my death rattle

I hear those same voices I will never meet saying
      I don't care if you die
      and my soul is clean

TIERRA

DIANA ANHALT

I pass an abandoned hacienda—
clock stopped at three fifteen—and enter
Zopilote, festooned in holiday tinsel.
Here shanties—their rebars topped

with empty bottles—line the side streets.
Political posters blanket walls
and an adobe hut slumps under the bulk
of a satellite dish. Discarded tires,

scrapped cars, huddle in vacant lots.
In front of the church, doors patched
in tin, a slim green plot, a few poinsettias.
Stubs of grass sprout like yesterday's whiskers.

A woman kneels. Head lowered, she removes
dead leaves from an azalea, buries her hands
in soil, sprinkles water from a coffee can.
Does she work for you? I ask the priest.

No, but once she owned a plot of land.
Tells me her footprints are furrowed deep
in its soil. She comes here to remember.
Does no harm.

Back When We Were Dirt

Amy Baskin

We knew our place.
Grounded ourselves to farms with our husbands' names.
Welcomed earthworms to house themselves within us.

Baked ourselves into bricks, sidled up one against another
until we made floors and walls, slopped on clapboard
with our connective tissues of clay.

We bettered ourselves with sand and gypsum, absorbent sponges.
Took it all in with room for minerals and molecules alike,
breathed air into the folds of our nostrils and realized we were alive.

We cultivated ourselves gravid only when we chose
to manifest as arable land. We welcomed the challenge
of tight spaces, parameters in which we carried

our complex creations,
formed proteins, and acids, gave footing to
nurslings, and knew deep down nothing good

could grow from moldboard plows tamping us
down to hardpan. Somehow we have forgotten
and let slide that we were always the foundation.

Nimble Flies

Lauren Camp

Today I crushed 82 flies against windows,
letting them fall in arcs. Devout in the dull noise
and scattershot effort, I tissued the panes of splattered juices
and transparent black wings. Oh, I couldn't stop
hating the swirl and plague of those insects. Always more
to put down to the sill—more bounty, more
spectacle, more shuddering. Though my love was there, I was alone
in my depraved heart and my thrashing—
a territory I had the audacity to ooze. Of course,
I knew there is nothing to be done
about Baltimore, Ferguson, Charleston, about every
ghetto corner, homicide, every extermination. Stupid me,
thinking my slashes of motion and trample
could fix the sticky noise of anything
when the country is flung to an enormous composition
of rough and long textures of flat black sadness.
Who had allotted the flies?
I kept moving my wrist. My husband gently made soup
as I bruised every edge of our beautiful house.
He moved out of the way of my dramatic spread, my despair
and surge to keep smacking. To free myself
from any wrong connotations in this violent glory,
I only tallied the clumps: segments
and legs. Still thrilled in the explosion of leftover
lines, I turned back to my love whose blue eyes can hold
the legacy and devastation of faraway clouds.
The failure of innocence is that it ends.
More nimble flies hopped on the glass.

Large Contrast Examples

Lauren Camp

Even in this breaking world, the small skulls came out
in peace last night, gathering sweets.

Ululant crows crowded the phone lines.
All the littles kept saying thank you thank you—the barest

amount of immensity
in this slight town with its cursive snakes and starlight.

∾

One day I took the man who prays within me
through glass-dashed concrete walls under hawk-scowl

and aspens. On a dead end, everything
was salvaged: lavish vista, a valid palace. Lost within it, we turned

and found an older woman fallen beside her blue
truck. What did we lift? Bones, bruises and canes.

None firmly in place. Only a temporary parsing.

SORRY CITY SWEETLY

LAUREN CAMP

The city lifts the bottom—midweek always—tar, brick, fog
fighting its damp dirge. All bodies holding
or shoving particular gestures.

Up from the grate, bourbon-riddled squatters perch
in their whispers. Everywhere the scent

of diesel, a hooded sun. Our bus moves its exasperations,
seat by seat, crosstown, where it enters and exits
the tunnel. A woman sobs. And then, in a get-along, get-along, we're slapped
to the street between currents

of glass, our view trimmed to reason of skyline.

At the park, enthusiastic pigeons trail their utopian vestiges,
and we stroll their departures where sewage splays
in grim crevices. Where an unsorted man coughs

his mournful heartbeat in a black garbage bag. The allowable homes
of some humans—we notice

the liminal states of erasure, and give them more
room for their bearing. On the subway, we hear thick wavering
ribbons of crisp pitted slurs till we stop

for liver and syrup with sections of crisped chicken. Gristle
between teeth. And back to upright
night shadows. Architectural angles. Token, token, again all sides

a stampede. Nothing more silencing than the roar

of each cross through the city. Than the tender folded
shoulders of strangers. And slowly, we hear what is hardly audible: a man
with gold crown pulling delicate music from slender
strings on an old violin, the platform layered with glory

instead of resistance as the train comes in
screaming. Only then can we lift to street level and even more
congestion, to neon that slips up from concrete, marking us radiant.

Here the Awful Happens Elsewhere

Lauren Camp

Pretend
the turning is

sorrow & we are lost in our talk
without profile.
Here the awful happens

elsewhere—

the dismembered
children in Gaza.

Ebola or the Jihadis.

We are managing the hurt
with our grimaces. We're still working

or running or climbing—swift,
never ceasing. This discipline

releases us
from feeling

angry.

English Lessons

Sarah Carleton

Her words in Arabic translate as
I love you more
according to a bilingual friend—

confirmation that the mom and I adore each other.
Normally, we garble sign language—
hand to heart, hugs and kisses

—and rely on pictures for vocabulary.
Last week I brought cookbooks,
and now the kids can say *soup, rice, strawberries.*

We learned that *hamburger* and *kabob*
are the same in both languages.
Olive oil made her eyes light up,

sent us all chattering, miming and googling
till we arrived at consensus.
"You have an olive tree," I said.

"Yes, yes! I have a tree in Syria."
She pronounces it "Sooria"
so it sounds susurrous like the name

of the beloved. In this living room
her tree exists in present tense.
We'll stay away from past tense for now.

The Guardians

Sarah Carleton

Mornings, I peer between fog patches
on the windshield
and brake behind yellow buses,
my son locked in heavy metal
and dream anxieties.
Bent-leg girl shleps across the avenida,
too slow for the light.
A hunchback posted by the overpass
watches us stop and start.

Clouds bloom operatic
and flamingo pink
over the Floridan building
while below, small braided citizens
in checkered knapsacks skip
from one sidewalk to the next,
a giddy zip that buoys my mood
like a sunrise.

Stationed at corners
all over the city,
women in neon vests direct
the flight patterns of kids.
For weeks after the bad election,
the sky was grimy and electric wires
hummed with dread,
but the crossing guards ignored all that
and kept halting traffic with palms forward
like waterbenders throwing forth walls of ice.

Miami Airport Nocturne

Sarah Carleton

These places are always so hushed.
Even that child bouncing from chair to chair

makes subsonic waves. His parents open their mouths
and release undetectable scolding into the tank.

Spanish sounds like bird chatter
in the pocket of a wool coat,

the middle range tamped down. Suitcases roll, roll
without a hitch on endless terrazzo mirrors.

The lack of definition stupefies. I dream open-eyed
until a group of women draped in yellow

salwar kameez and headscarves
shine their excitement at the arrivals gate.

Suzanne

Patrice Claeys

*"...there are children in the morning
They are leaning out for love..."*

—Leonard Cohen

There, spooning lemongrass soup, her ten
slender years calm amid the bustle of waiters,

the air bright with ginger, so steamy it fogs her glasses,
she sits. There, like her name-song, she stops the heart.

In her innocence, she searches for her mother,
each thin-wristed woman a candidate, touchstone

to identity. She trawls the shops, scans family tables
at restaurants on Argyle Street. She has chosen Vietnam

for her class project, mysterious land that claims
a quarter of her blood. Her eyes rove the market displays

of long green pods and sacks of tarnished gold spices.
Everything scented, strange. In one shop she alights

on a miniature scene—dark carved figures leading oxen,
carrying bundled sticks, toting tiny swinging buckets

from yoked shoulders. A village. Nearby a seated divinity,
tasseled triangles ascending to shiny points of colored tinsel.

The owner approaches. We tell him she has made her display board
of facts and pictures but now needs souvenirs, food, small tokens

from the county. He offers her, on loan, the tiny figures.
No names or numbers exchanged. *Good karma,* he says.

When you return them, we will both be blessed.

We buy child-sized wooden shoes, dried dragon fruit,

two shallow interlocking baskets—the country's version of a lunch box.

He wraps each fragile, intricate figure in tissue, smiles and bows.
Her phantom mother becomes both more and less.

Park of Human Rights, Izmir

Roger Craik

Outlandish by the sea,
it stands declarative:

Insan Haklari Parki

open for you and everyone
to saunter round its gardens,

regard the three colossal
slabs of marble arches

justified by lists of men
who fell in wars, or died of wounds.

The chiseled legend reads
"her insan uzgur."

(All humans are free.)

From these structures in this park,
a black gigantic spike,

goes slanting, high and deep

above the forced-in shrubs, the walkways
frozen hot in ripples, up

over the Aegean, the living sea.

But if your eye
sidles back down to where the spike begins,

it'll snag
a clumsy barricade of wire

to pierce, to stripe
that urchin whose one aim

is climbing climbing climbing

past that black and red
skull and bones

—YASAK—

and higher, up to the spot
where he'll stand and point and laugh and mock.

No explanation is given of the spike.
No explanation is given of the wire.
No list of names depends on either.

GHOSTS ON THE CENTER LINE

SARA COMITO

A divided highway, and the travel
                posters never feature the payday

loan center, a woman in Haitian
                colors flowing in that palm tree

breeze, hand cupping the darkened
                window. Stepping back, it's a mirror

    of loss and generosity.

    She might be sick for home. Or I am.
Poverty is not more exotic the closer

                you get to the equator, pedestrian
        safety never much improved.

    Strollers at the overpass containing someone's everything
    for a nap under the bridge. Or wielded in lieu of a crosswalk
    as innocents rest their heads.

This is a crisis at no border. South is Miami.
~

    The landed homeless think most of all of their precious carts, so the deputy
    was mystified to find a paper ream of paint chip samples among Gloria's cargo,

abandoned.

        What space did she have to renovate besides between her ears?
                Turns out, that's where the future lives.

Company Town

Sara Comito

Beyond the field of monarda and sleeping bees, the foundry
fire glows false sunrise. Chuck-will's-widows—all male—
slide-whistle across the night one-to-another their
useless lament. A weathervane rooster, fed on
dust, creeks a click toward north to crow
about rust. 12 souls were lost when
the particles conspired to combust. The
papers talk ventilation and liability. Slats stop
moaning as the rocking chair slows—my sister is
done with this feeding. When the screen door slams, I'm
watching the foundry smolder, considering the long night ahead
for my nephew.

Emily as the Bird Falls

Darren Demaree

The dark doesn't brighten.
The wings move light until they don't.
Emily keeps things dark

until she tastes the moisture
in the mud beneath her. I wait for her
in that mud. How glorious it is

to see how long she keeps her wings
tight to her body. I am teased
more often than not,

but there are occasions where
she abandons all flight
to just land amidst the dirt

that has been found by the rain
& by me, the one who calls for her
with words that are no song at all.

CIGARETTE BRUISE

Anuja Ghimire

In the flat by the street, I watch the city from the second story window
a small goods store for each day's small needs
enter policeman
enter a boy, few inches smaller
man in uniform points at cigarettes with his baton
boy in unremarkable cotton points at puff with his index finger
It was the time of revolution and overthrowing
the sun still above the pear tree
constable's hands on the boy's shoulders for leveling
boy's body on the cement floor
black boots on the boy's face
world watches watchman kicking
street gatherers scatter like moths after suffocating light
boy doesn't bleed or break
man with two lit cigarettes in his mouth blows the smoke to me

CITY GIRL GOES CAROLING IN THE VILLAGE

Anuja Ghimire

I once was the city girl, the teacher's niece from Kathmandu
one with clean, white skirts, canvas shoes and tennis rackets
the first week no child in the village came near me or the air I brought on the night bus
how I'd watch all the girls who walked just like me and laughed with friends
in the night of the singing and dancing, my first yawn and a girl accused me of my fancy ways
"drop her off, she's a loss," as if I couldn't hear her whispers to my cousin
who tried to hold my hand and guide my feet to the next house lit with oil lamps
but I couldn't open my eyes in the ennui, the dark air still filled with heat
and the girls who hated me carried my limp body home as if to a funeral

Mourning in America

Patrick Hansel

B will ride the bus to school today,
backpack on her lap, earbuds humming
with Daddy Yankee and Luis Fonsi.
She will explore particle theory,
themes of loss and duty in Shakespeare
and Garcia Marquez, the effects of
wage and price controls in post-
war America. At lunch, she will
laugh at stupid jokes, check Snap
chat and Facebook, text a friend
from her summer course at a well-
known college. After the final bell,
she will ride the bus home, have
a snack, walk to her little brother's
bus stop, watch Youtubers, start
on homework, wait for her parents
and dinner, more homework, her
favorite TV show on Netflix, bed.
Somewhere in there—though
Google and Amazon and Apple
decry it, oppose it, the President
of these United States will act
on her fate, though he does not
know her, or know any path to gain
that knowledge. Whatever he says,
it will be about greatness, but
B and the 800,000 will know
it is about the hunt. After she
brushes her teeth and slips
into bed, perhaps she will
hum the song as she hugs
her pillow, her college, her life:
Despacito. Despacito.

A Day Without Immigrants

Patrick Hansel

You would not see M's
beautiful smile, or hear B's
crazy laugh. The steak would be
burned because D had not
cooked that day, the flowers
would wilt and the tomatoes
wither, since L had not risen
early to water. The boxes
would not be packed by T,
nor the parts assembled by J.
The penne with marinara
and the chicken almond ding
and the filet mignon would not
be served by A, M & B, nor
the floors mopped by R.

Your sod would not be cut
and your roofs nailed on
without A through H;
the diapers of our elders not
changed by I through P;
and the mouths of our
toddlers would not be fed
by Q through Z. And yes,
the altar cloths would stay
stained and dusty because A
had not washed, ironed and
lovingly laid them on the wood
as a nest for the body,
the blood and the word.

Yes, they all have voices.
Yes, they all have names.
I will not write them here,
citizens. Some of you have

ears connected to the heart,
but some of you have ears
connected to the whip.
Who will listen to whom?

The Midfielder Bows Down for Prayer

Patrick Hansel

It has rained three days straight,
and the Blackhawks are itching
to get back on the pitch. There's
only so much waiting that feet
can stand. I drop my daughter
and the other two girls
off at the edge of the away team's
field, and park the car under
an unknown tree. Heat has ramped
up humidity, and steam rises off
the grass like incense.
As warmups conclude, N asks
me where she can pray—it is
that hour, and each bit of earth
that is not mud is wet grass.
I am not her coach, nor
her father, but she trusts me,
perhaps because I drive her
to each practice and match,
my daughter and the others
laughing with her in the back seat.
I reply, "wherever you can,
I guess," and she removes her
jacket, lays it on the ground,
kneels on it, and bows towards
the East. Her hijab touches
the blades of grass that sparkle
with the remnant of heaven.
The ref's whistle blows
as she rises. She smiles
and nods to me, the little
cousin of a bow, and takes
the field with the other ten.
Soon their feet will dig

up pieces of earth like
buried treasure, soon the ball
will fly, soon I'll shout
"Pass the ball, N,
damn it, pass the ball!"

The "John School"

Jennifer Jean

This Baptist basement has low ceiling tiles.
Every man looks like his online mugshot.
Known.
Some everyman

cognitive therapist gets up, says, *The world
is like a checkerboard
where buckets of crap occasionally
crash down
from the sky.** He cackles. Motions.

About a hundred guys stir,
creak on a hundred fold-outs—every numb butt shifting.
Some guys doodle.
They cross and uncross
sneakers, loafers,
on pencil shavings. On loosed tobacco.

Then it's: here comes
the urologist
in scrubs. He's got charts. *God…*
someone moans. Loudish.

A few men
scratch something. Scratch
the next thing. The itch
just moves around to another patch of skin.
Then "Alexis,"

fresh from a factory
job, booked 80 plus times and
shot while hooking,
gets up, says, *You're not so different*

as me.

Her small face is wrinkle-free
under a wool purple hat,
Everyone has to look

at the void
they're trying to fill.

Someone's wife gets up, says, *Gonorrhea,*
to the man-
crowd. Her man
got 5 to 7 with that curse.

And now, I can't... she says

looking down at an ant
hefting a crumb across the concrete,
while her audience thinks, *Shit!*
or *She knows...*
or *Just finish.*

A few guys don't blush.
A few do.

* "Every school seeks to be a bridge between no-knowledge and knowledge. A "John School" is meant to act as a bridge between: purchasing a human, and ceasing to purchase a human due to understanding the harm that purchasing causes that human, the buyer, and society.

*The dialogue from the "cognitive therapist" is a direct quote from Nashville's John School director Kenny Baker in an interview with NPR in 2011: https://www.npr.org/2011/05/24/136617710/john-school-teaches-about-ills-of-sex-solicitation

Ode to Fast Willie and Friends

Allison Joseph
—Fitzgerald Comics, 1976

How come I never knew
about Fast Willie Jackson and crew,
a chocolate-coated version of *Archie* comics
straight outta the ghettofabulous no-cale
of MoCity USA, where the Man was represented

by a single blond-haired bullnecked honky cop
too corny to give anything but litter citations?
This broke-ass comic book
could have given me role models
funkier than Betty and Veronica, like Dee Dee—

foxy in her multicolor hiphugger bellbottoms,
round-the-way girl in hoop earrings.
She knew she was fly, beautiful and black
all her life, which only existed for seven issues
in 1976. I could have felt pride

in the burgeoning pimposity
of Frankie Johnson, blueprint for future playas,
so slick he comes to Dee Dee's birthday party,
reaps all her presents, then splits for another
sister's pad, 'cause that girl's birthday

is next week! I could have seethed in rage
with righteous Jabar, scowling with protest placard
and beret, though his first protest should have been
against these lame plots, jive characters—like
the unnamed shaggy-haired hipster white boy

who solely existed to answer "Yes, I can dig it!"
to Fast Willie's existential "Can you dig it?"
At nine, would I have been able to smell
the stench of opportunism of this whole
draw-it-black-and-they-will-come operation,

this phenomenon in multicultural clownism?
After all, this was a whole city of happening
brothers and sisters, groovy as they wanna be,
decked in platforms, dressed like Huggy Bear's
left-back cousins. Instead of Jughead, they had

Jo-Jo, clear rip-off of J.J. from *Good Times*.
Instead of Moose, they had Hannibal. Sometimes
no representation is better than any. So I'm glad
I never curled under my bedspread, flashlight in hand,
spellbound by teenspolitation in blackface,
30 cents an issue for a lifetime of stereotypes.

Too Many Houses

Allison Joseph

after "Living for the City"
by Stevie Wonder

My knees ache from years of kneeling, from my weight
on them as I scrub toilets in houses so fancy I still use
the back door, long after Rosa rode that bus. My back
aches from bending to pick up trucks and dolls, from
cleaning up after children I spend more time with than my own—

washing their underwear, clothes, cleaning their wastebaskets.
My shoulders, my neck, my legs, my feet—they all ache
from too many hours in too many houses, big fine mansions
where I'm not even allowed overnight in the maid's room.
When I go home, feet sore, uniform dirty, when I ride

the bus like Rosa did, I think of the last time I saw
my son, him so strung out he didn't know his own name,
shuffling and talking to himself like a crazy man, saying
he was so glad he left Meridian, mumbling, mumbling.
Weary, I turned my head to him, stared at this wild-haired,

red-eyed demon that was calling me Mama and said,
I don't know you. You ain't my son. Now, on this rickety bus,
with my tired feet and sweaty uniform, I know my son
could be dead, face down in a New York City gutter, needle
in his arm, or bullet through his head. And as I know this,

my eyes don't water, my throat doesn't ache. I don't cry
anymore because it's too hard, and all my body wants
is to lie in a bed no one else has slept in—not my husband,
not my daughter, not even my son, who doesn't—can't—
respect the woman who shined his Sunday shoes

brighter than anything we ever dreamed of.

Summer Sonnet in Orange

Jennifer Schomburg Kanke

Let the cosmos die, let each orange petal
turn over in the mower's blade, every leaf
left to blend and dry with the grass clippings.
You did not ask them to reseed out here,
didn't till and fertilize this hard ground
so they might let their roots find deep waters.
They will grow anywhere they land, it's true,
driveway crack or decaying red cypress mulch.
No, dig them up gently, fill yogurt tubs
and cleaned out jelly jars with potting soil.
Get enough root that every bud blossoms,
no leaves left withering and falling in the strong sun.
Call all your friends, run shoeless door to door,
Enough for all, enough for all, enough.

The Mullet

Jennifer Schomburg Kanke

Does he understand the choice?
That he's one of only a few who can live
in fresh or salt water, or does he swim
where he's born, taking on the taste of the salt
or mud, not knowing? Either place, he'll jump
from the waters in a shimmering arch and I'll think,
what a joyful fish. The fisherman says,
He's escaping a predator, baits the hook. The tour guide
says *Sea lice,* the force of the water the only thing to free him.
But it's none of those things. It's the oxygen.
Packed tight in large schools, they tire of competing to breathe,
tire of fighting for what they need and they jump, jump, jump
to get themselves a little more, though they know
they can't survive there for long.

To My Neighbor, Coughing Across the Street

Jennifer Schomburg Kanke

There is a companionable stillness
to the neighborhood in the dark mornings
when owls still call to each other,
but all the misplaced solar lights
have run their charges out hours ago.
Only a few of us are up, puttering
in the coolness we hope will stay.
We know that it won't, it never does.
Soon the sun will rise and with it
the temperatures, even as October arrives.
The houses will stir and fill
with the sounds of breakfast and busyness,
the things the world wants from us,
the things it will take without our say.

As If

Lynne Knight

for Forrest Hamer

I was reading his book the other night
when I came to the lines *As if all poems*
need to be written & I thought of the times
he & I used to meet for coffee to talk
about poetry. We were just starting out
again, both of us having kept silent

for over a decade, reasons as separate
as our lives. We regretted time lost,
thinking what we might be writing now
without the long break. Or that's what
I said. He listened, nodding, as his other
work had taught him to listen to patients.
Listen to patience, he might have said;

I saw such counsel in his eyes, being
directed inward. He was learning
to say what he had to say, to know
what was not his. As if one man
could speak for centuries of troubles.
As if history were no more than words

about what happened. As if the cries
on those slave ships could not still
be heard in silences long after—
tongues pressed down by the bit,
wordless defiance. As if listening
were not part of what is being said.
As if everything needs to be written.

THE TATTOO

LYNNE KNIGHT

Show her, he said. *Show her the tattoo.*
But his aunt shook her head, pulled the sleeve
of her sweater down past her wrist even though
it was August, oppressive Detroit heat. I stared
at the floor, back up at the sleeve. Her other
arm was bare, the sweater sleeve rolled above
the elbow. A pretty woman, with silver threads
through her black hair. Pretty, but sad, I saw,
as she stared out the window. My lover
wrote something in the notebook he kept
in his breast pocket, the seed bed, he said,
of the novels he would write. We were young,
I knew nothing of being forced to wander
in search of a land one could call one's own.
He put the notebook back, said something
to his aunt in German, causing her to put
her hands over her ears. I knew the basics:
the boots in the night, the hastily packed suitcase,
the train shunting back & forth while more & more
dead stood in the car. No one else in her family
survived. The tattoo could be surgically removed,
my lover told me, but she refused: it was all she had
to remind her of the evil in us all. He tried again
in German. His aunt took her hands from her ears
when he stopped & put them on his face, pulled it
to her own. *Such a terrible shame,* she said.
*You've been taught to think you can understand
anything if you find the right words.*
But there are no words for this.
You think you could make a novel of this?
Look, she said, pushing her sleeve up
and pointing to the number.
Only a monster would keep reading.

Northern Vermont

Rustin Larson

The mirror reflection
of the painting is all about the future.
We cannot live there.

Two women meet
on the road to Pissarro's
village. A little girl hides
behind her mother's skirt.
The cattle lie in the field.

When I was a child,
I walked these fields alone
never thinking of danger.

Tonight, I drank a pint of stout
and watched the ember
of my life glow, down there.

It was a winter's night
and embers were falling
from the sky and glowing

in the streets in vast
piles. The ember removal
team had to be called in

with their huge machine.
This was all quite close
to the Canadian border,

and everyone spoke softly
so as not to wake them, the Canadians,
who slept.

The Tunnel of Snakes

Rustin Larson

A woman in Australia
was bitten by a non-
venomous snake
who was living in her toilet.

The bite hurt,
and the woman was traumatized,
but no one died.

In India, however,
someone was bitten
by a very deadly snake.
The sun went down
like an expensive cocktail
at a dream resort
and never came back up.

Today in Iowa, the highway
is a snake of ice.
It flares orange
when the day combusts
and comes to a polite,
though dark, end.

Sewing lesson

Gisèle Lewis

Her blunt fingertips tremble, feed calico beneath the machine's needle.
The weary engine sputters and moans
as the Syrian woman lowers her foot to the pedal
so tentatively, as though the Singer may buck and gallop.
I hover, murmur encouragement.
Her layered scents—*oud*, rose—comfort me like someone else's lullaby,
and the warm, granular voice,
whose grandmother?
Tawny, timid, she shuffles
across a scuffed linoleum floor, crisscrossed by snaking extension cords.
No more, she says and shoos away the fractious machine,
spreads a dainty doily, then stacks homemade honey-and-pistachio delicacies,
brightening the squalid community center
into a dress-up Sunday parlor.
She has seen gruesome things, I think.
Handfuls of bland chintz should be no trouble?
Or shadowed by decimated fields of cotton, patterned in blood.

Halloween, 2016

Gisèle Lewis

The refugees are taking selfies in front of a poster
of the Statue of Liberty
whose patina-green dress and visor my child will wear
to trick-or-treat after dark.
Thank God for Snapchat filters—we are so much cuter now,
with pink kitten ears and whiskers,
experts in fatuous autobiographies.
"Spas, spas," the Kurdish mother exclaims and claps.
She unwraps
her hijab and hugs me
when I offer
hand-me-down fairy-princess gowns
to her sprightly daughters.
"Squeeze closer, everybody. Smile for the photo!"

The Billboard

Marjorie Maddox

"It's your word against our video,"
the billboard keeps flashing
as we rush past late one afternoon
on one of those highways that goes on forever
but not into *ad nauseam*, because true is still true
we want to believe, traveling circuitously
cross-country 100 miles an hour in our rented good will
with the hood down and our unbleached hair flying out behind us,
past the White House and Pittsburgh; past Dallas and *House of Cards;*
past *Oz, West World,* Hollywood; past childhood's *Twilight Zone;*
past prairie dogs popping like clockwork in and out of holes
dug all the way to China; past KGB pre-programed tumbleweeds
wire-tapping wind; past all these and back to the free
wild world of the badlands. Sure, you can ride with us.
It's a constitutionally alternative-options earth. Catch up. We're not
slowing down. Jump in.

Tiny Portraits of Men

Charissa Menefee

My daughter, barely in
elementary school, says,
while waiting at the table
for her supper:

"Girls can't be president."

When I ask why, she points
to the plastic educational
placemat in front of her,
covered in tiny oval portrait

after portrait after portrait after portrait after portrait after portrait
after portrait after portrait after portrait after portrait after portrait
after portrait after portrait after portrait after portrait after portrait
after portrait after portrait after portrait after portrait after portrait
after portrait after portrait after portrait after portrait after portrait
after portrait after portrait after portrait after portrait after portrait
after portrait after portrait after portrait after portrait after portrait
after portrait after portrait after portrait after portrait after portrait
after portrait after portrait after portrait after portrait.

Orchid Garden Residence Community

Cameron Morse

Sunrise crests the sixth-story balconies.
Bricks ridged to guide the blind run down the middle of the sidewalk
into a pole. Miscellaneous mandarin orange peels, sunflower shells,
cigarette butts scatter underfoot. Theo totters
around the compound, picking them up for the trash cans,
hands ruddy in the February wind.

Like my grandmother in Golden Acres, who culled curbside garbage
on neighborhood walks, who collected bags of walnuts
in the basement, an elderly woman stirs about in the shadows,
sorting garbage. When Theo approaches her dirty bucket,
she shoos his hands away. Here by invitation,
by the grace of an old friend, we pose,

globetrotters pretending to be Beijingers. The commissary boss
asks my nationality. We buy mulberries and quail eggs,
make believe. When afternoon sunlight levels with the second-story
window casements, grandmothers unpin clothes hung
between lamppost and tree trunk. Hedgerows harbor clumps
of snow like fugitives from the sun.

We visit the Summer Palace. Buy the obligatory map.
It says you're at the East Palace Gate, the Hall of Benevolence
and Longevity. It says Silver-Knuckled Wind, Theo
Hates the Harness with which you leash him.
Everyone admires his complexion. Smiles at the tantrums.

He darts about the Spacious Pavilion while Lili peruses
the gift shops. Stopping just short of the Seventeen-Arch Bridge,
we call it quits. Leave the wind
to wisp in the yellow shoots of lakeside willows.
Leave the magpies to cackle in their cypresses. Leave in favor
of an evening meal with friends, in favor of early bed.

Jetlagged and backpacked, we drag ourselves back
to Orchid Garden Residence Community below a liver-spotted gibbous,
the crackle of oil in the wok of an upstairs apartment.

Offerings

Cameron Morse

Headshots of the dead parents top a table
of offerings, a bucket of fried chicken,
a bowl of shrimp, red apples with brown spots.

It's not our apartment, so we steer away.
We steer Theo away from the space heaters,
the flat screen TV. Lin Lin reappears
in her tutu, a knot on her forehead
Grandma dabs with pig fat, the boisterous
auntie with a Peter Pan haircut.

After dark, streetlights emblazon Naping Road
with Chinese lanterns, a stream of colors,
caravan of bright lights, cavalcade
stretching beyond this ancient kingdom
of high rises to another dimension.
Dinner's cold by the time the last dish
hits the table, the last auntie arrives.

Baijiu warms the flushed uncles who sit long
getting drunk together in a swirl of women
and children. By now they know not to offer me rice
wine—rice or wine, for that matter—not to risk
another lecture on cancer and ketosis.

By the end of the evening a bowl of strawberries
appears. Theo has smeared six or seven globs
of the sugary goop on his chin, his bib
and apron, before we realize our children
have eaten offerings to the dead.

The Names of Children

Cameron Morse

I study the names of the children who surround me—*Lin*,
meaning forest. *Guo*, meaning fruit.
The morose uncle with uremia motions for me to sit
beside the cast-iron stove, but I'm layered

too thick for burning coal. Sunlight gleams
for the first time since we arrive
in the milky white tiles of the apartment block,
a single blurry cloud like a smudge upon the lens.

I hand over my pen and Guo Guo scratches out a page
in my knockoff Moleskine. I write around her hairy black mass,
increasingly banished to the margins. Aunties ask
what the hell I'm doing. My wife explains, *collecting*

material for poems. Lin Lin offers me a kernel of candied popcorn.
I decline. Aunties urge me to try the tofu,
beans and potato. Lili explains *cancer cells love glucose*.
Her aunts complain, *he can't eat anything*.

Coyote Oblivion

Bruce Pemberton

There's a dead coyote pup,
so I stop to pull it off
the edge of the road,
and set it in the tall grass,
sparing it the usual high-
way blood and guts.

I've never been this close
to one, dead or alive, have
had them in my yard at five
in the morning, but they've
always run off at the sight
of me.

Maybe he crossed the high-
way behind his mother, didn't
have her speed yet, so he
catches someone's fender,
or sets off on his own too soon,
without her counsel regarding
the hard ground and those
bright lights. She'll miss him,
sense his absence, then memory
will fade, as she births again
in the spring.

I'm able to pet his clean, soft
head, certain that no one's
ever done that or ever will.

Iraq, September 2004

Bruce Pemberton

In Memory of Sergeant Jacob Demand

We were both there, the same
time, with him up north in Mosul
and me in Baqubah, east of Baghdad.
I make it home in June and he dies
in September, five days after
his birthday.

His mother asks me to look
at his badges and ribbons, and
tell her what they mean. The
blue one with the wreath around
a rifle? I tell her how he earned
it. Those two ribbons at the top?
You know those, I tell her. That's
a Bronze Star and a Purple Heart.
I know, she says, just making sure.
He was such a good boy, she tells
me, too good, I should have expected
this. Just sports and homework, and
bed early, even, she says, on weekends.
He ships out for basic training two
weeks after graduation, didn't even
give himself one last summer at home,
catches a bus up to MEPS, gets sworn in,
stays in a downtown hotel, swims laps
in their pool, and leaves his new goggles
poolside, for anyone who might want
them. In the morning, a military van
takes him to the airport for his first
flight ever.

The years vanish and he deploys all
over, calls his mother when he can,
mostly in the middle of the night,
her time. He has a month left in

Mosul, and almost likes it there.
They are on a foot patrol and
encounter an unexpected wall of bullets.
He's shot six times, but manages to
shield his interpreter and saves
him. They call in a medivac, but six
gunshot wounds from an AK-47
become a quiet trip home in a
transfer casket.

The small schools around here play
eight-man football and coaches have
to beg boys to play. He would anchor
the line, play center on offense and
nose guard on defense, then come
home and fall asleep in the tub.
C'mon, dear heart, wake up, his
mother would tell him. His father
would peer over her shoulder with
a beer and two aspirin. Swallow
these, and drink this, you've earned
it, he tells his son. You played your
guts out.

To Nelly Sachs

Claudia Reder

My metaphors are my wounds
—Nelly Sachs letter

Each of your poems is a pine cone
in forests all over the world.
Or: perhaps a torn piece of poem
fallen on a rock ledge or
settled near a field of lettuces.
Someone may lean over to tie
a shoe and read it.
This year you are 127 years old.

If I believed in alchemy
I would look for you, a lost sister,
in Stockholm, or immured
near your homeland, Berlin,
wondering where you would be welcome.

On seeing a photograph of
your study, I imagine you seated
at the typewriter in front
of the window. While I read
your poems, new roots form,
new languages I didn't know possible.

The night is made of rivers.
I swim hand over hand until night ceases
and the stars are grey blue.
The brightest thing is the starflower
dancing on the water.

Now your hands are leaving you.
Like children, they need more space.
Come sit in my crowded kitchen.
Sip some cloud soup.
We toast: To life, L'Chaim.
We pass the poems on to the next generation.

For A Day I Stop Talking

Amy Small-McKinney

Though I think about my father
fired from his job when they found out he's a Jew.
Think about my brother, thrown from his bicycle, a *dirty Kike*.
A friend's aunt complaining how the Jews
were taking over her shoreline.
She didn't know   I am one.
Riding in a farmer's truck, loving the long pale Iowa fields,
until he complained Jews were taking over his countryside.
He didn't know   I am one.
How only yesterday
I begged my daughter to take off her Hebrew
necklace, here in America,
when riding a train or bus or walking down
our streets filled with tempting shop windows.
I am searching for reason's language.
Instead find the formless clay-beast, my own *golem*,
I thought buried long ago, sacred words stuffed in her mouth,
she is gnawing to get out, furious. She is afraid.
Beneath the family stone, its carved hands triangular and touching,
my parents are waiting for me to explain.

July 2018

Alison Stone

Because politics can make kids anxious,
I say nothing to my daughters
as we stand on the roof awaiting fireworks
except how beautiful the sky looks
as cobalt bleeds into pink.
Twelve Thai soccer players stuck in a cave.
Media fixation—the danger! The oxygen!
Activists were told not to protest outside
facilities where children wait in cages,
our well-intentioned chanting
just another flavor of terror.
The heroic divers! The forecast of rain!
The roof deck is crowded.
The detention centers are crowded.
So much red, white, and blue.
As the finale begins, a thick
cloud drifts over the blossoming light,
moving like an eclipse until
only a sliver is visible.
Boats honk in the bay. The boys and their coach
rescued! Half the migrant kids under age five,
court-ordered returned to their families,
haven't been. The parents difficult to locate,
some deported. The boys invited, but too weak,
to attend The World Cup. Teary, I pack
my daughter's trunk for camp. Two weeks. Protein
bars, water shoes, extra sunblock. I'll write
every other day. A barefoot one-year-old
compelled to represent himself in court.
My privileged grief.

Living in the "Birthplace of the Neutrino"

Barrett Warner

Last night's four mile walk before fish supper
took us down one of the many dirt roads
(too many springs in these parts for asphalt)
and we passed a five-year-old girl sitting by the side.
Ignoring my dogs, the girl just looked at me, said,
Hey why are you walking down this road?
I said, *Exercise!* But you know, it did affect me.
A few weeks ago, for Martin Luther King's birthday,
I took the dogs to the countryside, told myself
we'd hike until we found slave cabin ruins. Thinking
it might take a week, all of us were disappointed
we only had to walk a half hour to find remains:
gray and brown boards clinging to shotgun beams,
the sadness staving off the rot like resin and oil.
You can't always hear time and distance, can't always
hear lost African saints singing up from the depths
of history, but down here you don't have to squint
to see it. It's there, it's all around us, I guess.

Like the gray marker as you come into town
which glamorizes the birth of the neutrino,
in 1954, the year of the *Brown v Kansas* decision.
The neutrino is a small particle that is neither positively
or negatively charged, contrary to popular electrons,
and is the product of radioactive decay,
which is like decay that is so intense
it's radioactive. What's more, its parents—two men—
had to wait 40 years before being posthumously
awarded the Nobel Prize in Physics, causing quite a stir
in our sphere of twice-blooming azaleas and pine straw.
We now sport a neutrino statue, and a museum
of the neutrino, and a parade up Weak Forces Avenue
which coincides, not coincidently, with the Re-Enactment
of the Battle of Aiken—a minor skirmish. The local spin

is that it nearly turned the outcome of the war.
What is the matter—what *is* matter—if something
can go right through it like it didn't exist?

Reviews

Reviews

IF THE HOUSE
by Molly Spencer

REVIEWED BY ELIZABETH NICHOLS

Inside Molly Spencer's chapbook, *If the house*, readers discover that "There's / A place inside the body that can't forget, / A room where various pasts pick at the bones." Physical spaces like *room* and *house* undergo a poetic transmutation into the interiors of human heart and mind, revealing the speaker's inner-most, hidden self. The past eclipses into the present with routine actions like the snapping of beans and the peeling of oranges, imbuing the seemingly mundane with startling poignancy. Rich, potent imagery allows the reader to feel the pathos lurking just beneath a fragile veneer of domesticity. Spencer's collection transports the reader to a liminal world where metaphor, simile, and stanza divulge that a suppressed inner turmoil has bled into waking life. Spencer's *If the house* takes the reader on a journey into the speaker's psyche where the house is at once literal and figurative, and the boundaries between the physical and the imagined are erased.

The journey begins with one foot stuck in the sands of the past. In the poem "Bridging," the past melds so seamlessly with the present that speaker has trouble distinguishing between the two:

> ".... Inside the house,
> the shadows have their way, ink brimming
> into the contours of life, bone-black
> shapes of table, lamp, eventual silhouette
> of your father, backlit in the window as you sit
> together remembering...
> ...it was the rowboat, wasn't it? It was
> raining. No,
> it's you daughter
>
> in the back seat saying, *Tell me a story*."

Tension between the past and present, which are represented by summer and winter, respectively, is ever-present in *if the house*. "Look back," says the speaker, "and everything stands / for something." Throughout the collection, when the speaker looks back into the past she sees a little girl. The girl repeatedly appears in Spencer's poems, and she is accompanied by the sights and sounds of summer. The speaker describes an almost halcyon existence where the little girl—her past self—lives in the light of a perpetual golden hour: "When I was a girl / it was always summer. The sand stayed warm past dark and the lake, too." At the end of her story, the speaker tells her daughter that, "The girl / is still there hovering / over the scene, outcast, witness, wavering / angel—whether to be water, / whether to be a bridge." In essence, the speaker is saying that a part of her is still living in the past. In "Meadow: A Reckoning," The speaker tries to warn the girl that the verdant summer will wither into an adulthood of icy winter:

> "Girl, you have burned yourself out. Goldenrod
> Rusts at your edges, the dazed sky sharpens
> Its blunted blade toward blue.
>
> …
>
> Girl, you won't feel a thing. The meadow will
> Lie down. The first snows hardly ever stick."

Indeed, in sharp contrast to her summery past, the speaker's adulthood is marked by repeating images of snow, ice, and cold. "Just look," the speaker bemoans, "at what these winters have done / to me. Here I am / standing on the snow where it has fallen / thick over the creek and   crusted." She continues in "Elegy Beginning with a Text from My Brother, she describes the snow as a "season come down upon me," the snow a field she woke in with her "heart gone to windbreak." Winter has encased the speaker, rendering her life frozen in unfulfilling domesticity. It is no wonder that to escape from her iced-in present, the speaker looks to the warmth of her past: "In winter / a dreamed-of house is almost as good as a real one."

In her poems titled "Conversation," Spencer deftly communicates the strained relationship between the speaker and her partner. It is this strained relationship that largely characterizes the endless winter that the speaker's adult life is imprisoned in. In "Conversation with Shower and Vestibule," the dialog between the speaker and her partner is devoid of punctuation, and their words bleed into the imagery surrounding them: "From his side of the bed he says how do you feel / …She could answer but she is / Thinking about… / How the heat bore down like a long dull labor and / The thick air clung wet to her skin… / Like regrets he says are you sleep again." This blending of dialog and imagery reflects the confused, jumbled attempts of the couple to communicate with each other. It also underscores the mutable reality at work in *If the house*. In "Conversation with Windows and Green, the speaker's partner asks, "Why / Can't you just be happy." The partner's question recalls the haunting caws of the crows in the poem "Disclosures: If you are aware of any nuisance animals such as crows, chickens or barking dogs:"

> "The crows will go on gathering
> Inside you. The crows will repeat
> and repeat their hooked songs….
>
> The crows will creak and rasp
> like hinges. You'll wake to
> days that stain your hands, bits of char
>
> from a beach-fire, some forgotten summer. Days
> that, like the crows, want answers….
>
> The crows will follow you home wanting to know
> *are you happy now are you   happy*"

The speaker answers her partner, and the crows, with poetry. Well-crafted musicals follow a key formula: characters transition from speaking to singing at emotional peaks, and then break into dance at the crescendo of their overflowing feelings. Similarly, the speaker in *If the house* has reached a point where speech cannot convey what she is feeling, and is compelled to express herself with poetry. The lost, idyllic summer of her childhood is remembered in the "bits of char / from a beach-fire" on her hands, and the ice holding her in a sedate domesticity is cracking: "the ice is strong / Enough to hold you until it's not then you break / Through to another father world." She is overcome with the need to tell her story—the meaning she sees in windows and narrow, empty vestibules—even if her partner cannot or will not understand. She tries to share the meaning of "How the rough stones speak / Of the body," and why the "green insistent pull of river / Over skin" begets a deeper kind of knowledge than the shore—the shore that is "an edge felt in the body." Amid her partner's confused questions and dismissive responses, the speaker waxes about "distances / How they start with ordinary things silk / Over skin even a thin silk the inevitable shift / Of sand during storm." But the distance between the speaker and her partner cannot be breached: like sand blown inland by an angry storm it has grown into an impassable dune. "I have counted the all times / you didn't touch me," says the speaker, "Where / I have stood on shore / years and seasons, windward. / Don't pretend this sand was never stone." The speaker is trying to tell her partner his touch no longer has any purchase on the shores of her heart—that her life is frozen and she feels trapped inside herself—that she longs for the golden summers of the past to thaw the present and release her. In "Conversation with Shower and Vestibule," the speaker alludes to her longing for release when she says, "I am looking for a room to walk away through." But, in the end, the speaker keeps her partner "from the loose raft of" her "sorrow," recognizing with pained resignation that "Love can't make a road end up at home."

The poems in *If the house* are the speaker's attempts to grapple with a sadness that lingers like a chill she cannot shake. She wants to be able to give and feel more than the "small gray stone / of [her] sorrow." These poems are disclosures, elegies, litanies, and meditations that plumb the depths of her memories and experiences, looking for meaning in and release from a seemingly perpetual winter of discontent. It is as if, with a delicate press, the speaker pushes back a gossamer curtain hanging in her house and reveals an inner truth along with the window. With self-discovery, the speaker starts to feel the ice around her crack. But the spring waiting just beyond winter "unravels / the plot line," and does not seem to bring the relief the speaker is looking for: "The trees look sickly. The roadkill, / which the snow had covered, gleams again like a used womb." The numbing cold of winter is gone, but the speaker is left with new, uncovered pain that must be acknowledged. But, Spencer does not leave the collection or the speaker without hope. In the penultimate poem, "How to Love the New House," the reader is told to feel a new house "With both hands / In the arched darkness / On the stairwell / On your hands and knees / Until you ache with it / For the life of you / Until it shines." In the act of loving a new house, there is also a kind of self-love, a self-acceptance. In the end, the speaker turns to poetry to find hope: "I believe a single word can rescue." She sits at her table in her house "all through the slant / amber afternoon" and recognizes that "it is a table / I chose / again this morning:" winter has released its iron grip, and she can choose her mooring for the spring that will come.

Tunsiya / Amrikiya
by Leila Chatti

Reviewed by Linda E. Kim

There is a delicate unfolding of narrative in Leila Chatti's *Tunsiya / Amrikiya*. Chatti builds and re-contextualizes our understanding of the struggle to hold onto dual conflicting identities in America. The structure of her poetry collection is purposeful and keen. The poems create a crescendo arc of revelation, carefully placed in such a way so as to achieve the greatest emotional impact on the reader. In the reader's mind, the blank spaces of unsaid epiphany ferments in still waters of contemplation. Subtext deepens our understanding of the speaker's pain.

The poet's grasp on poetic techniques furthers our empathy. Lineation acts as a twist of revelations. Comma used as caesura has gravitas. Her enjambment draws sharp comparison between lines. Imagery is a comparative tool of beauty and despair. Metaphor is given the concrete weight of physicality. All these things help to capture the ambivalence of being a racial outsider in America.

The speaker draws us into her perspective and humanizes a foreign world. We experience the unique pain of alienation and isolation as she does. We understand the torment that is carrying a split national identity. *Tunsiya* is Arabic for Tunisian, female. *Amrikiya* is Arabic for American, female. The speaker is both in a post-9/11 world and has to somehow navigate this excruciating liminal space. It's a seemingly impossible position. She's trapped between two diametrically opposed cultures. Self-perception becomes distorted. Culture, family, beloved childhood Tunisian memories—once a comfort, these comes under siege:

> My mother thought her blood
> might protect us in this country
>
> from this country, her fair genes and cast-
> aside Catholic god. Thinks now
>
> she failed us as children

The question of race and religion wars within her. The white fair skin of her mother clashes with her "father brown and speckled." Secular pop culture and suburban mundanities grate against the pious murmurs of Muslim ritual, prayers, and faith. Americana threatens to overwhelm and subsume her. *Tunsiya / Amrikiya* is a study of contrasts, the poetry performative in its precarious balancing act.

In the poem "Muslim Christmas" the young speaker examines gifts left under an imitation Christmas tree. It bears "false twigs" and "copper wire arms." It rests on an air hockey table and is a "false icon," an "altar / of the unbelieving." It's a pretense that makes her mother weep. The speaker only sees "Santa Christ, Saint Jesus" as a marvelous figure, but this absurd conflation of God, Jesus, and Santa Claus only emphasizes the painful crack in her assimilation.

The speaker's daily existence is an exhausting exercise to reconcile two worlds. Her only respite is in language, in holding tight to that multi-faceted joy of linguistic art and human connection. Foreign tongues evoke the nostalgia of youth and the intimate joy of secret languages. Yet in America that same intimacy creates a barrier of foreignness, of alienation, of the Other. It's an acute dissonance the speaker is keenly aware of:

> ...Sometimes, I thought
> my father was a god, I loved him that much. And the news thought
> this was an impossible thing—a Muslim girl who loved her father.
> But what did they know of my heart, or my father
> who drove fifty miles to buy me a doll like a Barbie
> because it looked like me, short brown hair underneath her hijab,
> > unthreatening
> breasts and feet flat enough to carry her as far as she wanted
> to go?

By confronting our assumptions, the speaker challenges biases formed against the Muslim Other. There is a fierce and unapologetic pride in her reveal. In her reverence and observation of religious beliefs, she is unashamed. She says of "Fasting in Tunis":

> My God taught me hunger
> is a gift, it sweetens
> the meal. All day, I have gone without
> because I know at the end I will
> eat and be satisfied. In this way,
> my desire is bearable.

There is a hunger in her, both literal and metaphorical, to decrease any distance to her God. There is beauty in piety, in obedience to ritual and worship. Religious understanding helps to bridge the gap between human frailty and the greater metaphysical whole of God. She craves that connection. She intuits it'll lead to a resilience and strength to endure inner struggles.

But always death, trauma, and isolation beget shadows that grow. The speaker is greeted in America by "steely guns and colder eyes." She bears the loneliness of suspicion. In such an environment, it is difficult to hold onto faith. Darkness looms large as angered, unanswered prayers are cast into the void:

> In the dark I try every language you might
> recognize, but nothing calls you back;
> the words hang in the air, their own
> brief phantoms. The ocean offers
> no solace; I stand at its black edge
> as it retreats, draws close, backs away again.

And in the wake of 9/11, communities are further sundered. Violence so profane threatens to collapse all human understanding. In a perversion of holy faith, words of prayer have instead become weapons, a hateful rallying cry: "How many times have I felt / shame at those words—*Allahu / akbar*—felt it twist / like a knife inside me?" In the face of such emotive hate, people are speechless. Language has failed to protect. The failures and inadequacies of language become clear. It is the "joint failure of language / and prayer." It engenders a legacy of hate. It becomes almost too much to bear.

But poetry steps in as a way to process such grief when all other linguistic paths fail. She becomes reacquainted with prayer as faith becomes her refuge. In her father, she finds "his god and tongue." She finds beauty in piety and gains the strength to bear that anguished question of identity.

In seeking God, she finds him as natural and inevitable as landscape and nature. The sun, sky, and ocean are his domain. She is drawn to blue waters, to the affinity she shares with her father. "Early light shears cleanly through, glints off / shells and shoals of pewter fish." The sea is vivacious with life and alight with joy. In realizing this, she finds the waters that reflect the light of her God to be an irrevocable comfort.

It's an unshakeable solace in the dark. There is more to life than death. Conviction is "the blue skin of horizon, surface / smooth as a bed's new sheet, everything still / and untroubled around us, the ocean / parting gently as we enter, then sealing us in."

Blue carries her home. Traditional Tunisian architecture "commonly features large, ornate blue doors." The book's cover features one such beautiful door. Geometric and blue, it's a beacon of wood and stone. Such a door guides seekers and weary travelers home to the "blue mosaicked pool" of faith. In the speaker's journey to reconcile the two warring halves of her soul, she crosses the threshold of that door. And in the stillness of water, in the space of contemplation, she finds peace.

THE NUMBER 5 IS ALWAYS SUSPECT
by Bob Heman & Cindy Hochman

REVIEWED BY ELIZABETH NICHOLS

Bob Heman and Cindy Hochman's collection *The Number 5 Is Always Suspect* is a delightful showcase of wordplay and whimsy. This poetic collaboration exudes joy, reveling in word-craft, imagery, and the art of poetry. Heman and Hochman do not get lost in their repartee, however: they deftly blend their unique talents to create a new poetic voice. It is as if Heman and Hochman employed a kind of poetic numerology, divining meaning from each other's previous lines to create poems that are at once surreally beautiful and jarring in their impact. At times Seussian, at times introspective and somber, *The Number 5 Is Always Suspect* is a witty, fun romp in these poets' syntax-rich sandbox.

Poems 10 and 11 are perfect examples of the dazzling duality at work in the collection. Poem 11's playful imagery takes the reader through a Dali-esque series of questions that dive headlong into the poets' imaginations. At the same time, the questions are a tongue-in-cheek commentary on the meta-poem, or a poem about poetry:

"11.

Do you see a goldfish swimming through this poem?
Are there trees hiding behind the verbs?
Or maybe an adjective stuck between your teeth?
Does the meaning crawl away before you can examine it?
Do some of the words get lost in your thoughts?
Does the goldfish ever reappear?
Or turn unto a shark while you're deep in dream?

...

Or "very like a whale," as Polonius said to Hamlet?
What was it in this poem that he mistook for clouds?
The fact that in poems even sharks can turn cumulus?
How many clouds will you have to search to find the missing adverbs?"

In contrast, poem 10 on the page just opposite is completely different in its tone. Goldfish give way to the figures of Lazarus and Jesus, and images of zombie animals walking "the earth in peril and pain." Reminiscent of Dante's recollections of his tour through the underworld, the poem details Lazarus' disturbing memories after his resurrection. Of the afterlife, Lazarus recalls Jesus raising animals from the dead, but as nothing more than skeletons "not always recognized as they once were / defying the laws of evolution / but remaining a reminder of what we all will become / when the earth opens up and swallows us whole." The grim imagery is unexpected, and all the more impactful juxtaposed against its jocular neighbor, poem 11. But, despite the sudden shift in tone, poem 10 is not out of place in the collection. For, as poem 9 reminds the reader, "art is not for the faint of heart / sometimes it creeps up when least expected / and makes you go deep even when you're not ready."

In *The Number 5 Is Always Suspect* language is tangibly malleable, elastic. It yields like clay warmed in the poets' hands. Poem 4 begins with "the name of a fruit that was shaped wrong," but through wordplay the image kaleidoscopes and "the last line unfolds and new world begins." In poem 12, repetition reveals the character of "the house on the corner:" it "is repeated until it reaches the horizon," "is upside down," and finally "is no longer filled with words." The collection's reflection on words and language compounds into a discussion of poets and poetry. This is especially evident in poems 18 and 24. Poem 18 ruminates on the poetic process, and specifically on the building blocks of a poem, words:

> "the word was larger than the space it occupied
> it had nothing to do with fonts or fountains
> it was about the possibilities that lived inside
> and the people who dared to write about them
>
> …

> like ants we are always hungry for nourishing new words
> so we form colonies and march uphill in straight lines
> searching for the obvious and not-so-obvious
> peeking under crevices where language starts
>
> but sometimes what we find occupies no space at all
> and that's where inspiration begins."

The image of the industrious ant is particularly fitting for poets that worked together on The Number 5 Is Always Suspect, building poetry collection line by line as ants build a colony grain by grain. The wordplay of ants marching in a line compared to a literal poet's lines in poem is also apt. And, much like ants, poem 18 observes that words take up a small, finite space on the page, but can stand for concepts and build worlds much larger than themselves. The endless "possibilities that lived inside" words conclude with the discovery of new artistic ground for the poet "where inspiration begins." In the same vein, in poem 24 the reader finds "All of life open to interpretation." Like poem 18, poem 24 begins with a rumination on words, but then directly comments on the work of a poet: "And of course the words on the page can always be rearranged. / Or erased and patched together again. / Allowing the meaning to hide deeper, almost out of sight." In the end, it is the "up to the poets to tell us what we saw:" to make sense of the words, mine and combine for meaning, "even if it's only a bear waking from a dream."

Heman and Hochman's whimsical imagery, wordplay, and meta-poems combine in a uniquely evocative collection. Their collaboration celebrates language without losing sight of the joy and fun to be found in the process of creating poetry. The Number 5 Is Always Suspect demonstrates that, as in poem 18, their combined talents and voices have created a singularly new space where inspiration begins and thrives.

Prompts

Katie Chicquette Adams

Write about a vehicle you once owned, drove, or loved. Start with the objective truth of this vehicle—a description which could even be a list. Watch as the descriptions turn into quirky figurative language—and those into an unexpected comment about human life altogether.

Diana Anhalt

Every year family members return to the graves of their loved ones, decorate their tombs, bring food and drink. You, of course, would choose to leave a poem instead and would dedicate it to someone now dead—it doesn't have to be someone you know—but it could be an individual who has, in some way, inspired you.

Amy Baskin

Picture someone you can't stand, wet in a saggy bathing suit, on the cover of all the tabloids. Free-write about all the things you can't stand about that someone. Now picture that someone is your child and write some more.

Lauren Camp

Begin with "The pandemic has not yet finished." Include a color, a food and a wish.

Sarah Carleton

Find an audio recording of a poem in a foreign language that you don't speak or understand. Jot down what you think the poem is about just by the sound of it. Create your own poem from that.

Patrice Boyer Claeys

Take a poetry anthology and write down individual lines from various sources that grab your attention, being careful to record the poet next to the line he or she wrote. When you have a large enough collection (about 30 lines), begin moving them around, letting lines bump up against one another as you build a scene or convey an emotion. Keep assembling lines until you have made a cento, giving credit to contributing poets at the bottom of your work. Note: the rule of thumb is only one line per poet.

Sara Comito

Write a poem in two parts: the first is about your memory of a place from the past; in the second part, you revisit the place in present time. Make the last line of the first part become the first line of the second part.

Roger Craik

I find that it's very helpful to 'limber up' by doodling with a soft pencil, using my left hand always. This is what the British painter Frank Auerbach does. I also keep in mind a line by Sly and the Family Stone: "it's the truth that the truth makes it so alive." This sounds glib but it's true. There are any number of ways to convince yourself that what you are pleased with is good, but if your conscience tells you otherwise it is best to scrap it.

Darren C. Demaree

Write a poem holding an ice cube in your non-dominant hand, and edit the poem while drinking warm water.

Anjula Ghimire

Choose only one of your favorite poems that you have memorized. Begin your poem with the last word of your favorite poem. End the poem with the first word of your favorite poem.

Patrick Cabello Hansel

*Write a poem about an embarrassing incident in your life, and write it from the voice of **the last person on earth** you would want to tell that story.*

Jennifer Jean

Forgiveness is powerful—even when what's forgiven is a very small deed. Write a poem in which you forgive a very small deed from long ago. Write a poem in which you ask forgiveness for a very small deed from long ago.

Allison Joseph

Think of an object that you have or once owned. Describe it as if it were a person. Then describe it from the point of view of someone who is not you—a literary character, family member, cartoon character, etc. Then write a poem in the voice of that character—that chosen persona—speaking about this object.

Jennifer Schomburg Kanke

Select a role you play in your life and write a list of ten rules for doing it "right." Which of these rules would you break if you could? Write a poem that imagines the aftermath of breaking one or more of these rules. (Are the consequences more physical or mental? Could you live with them?)

Lynne Knight

Choose any word long enough to have many consonants and vowels in it. Starting with the first letter and going letter by letter, make smaller words from this word, and then use at least ten of them in a poem.

Example: rambunctious

rim, run, runt, rust, ram, rant, riot, arm, am, art, arts, act, action, ant, man, mar, mint, most, mist, must, bum, bus, bust, but, bun, burn, not, nib, nor, numb, cram, crust, cut, cub, cunt, curt, trim, tram, tomb, turn, imp, it, iamb, orb, oust, us, urn, sit, stir, storm, sum, sun, sub, suction, stub, sot, sort

There are enough words here for at least two poems, so for the second one, choose one of the words as your title—Tomb, Storm, Mist, Numb—and, using ten words (some can repeat, but at least half have to be different), write a poem with that title.

(This exercise works well on sleepless nights, too. If you're being kept awake by a problem or concern, try it—you'll drift into sleep before you finish finding all the words.)

Rustin Larson

My daughter Sarah gave me a wallet-sized journal in 2017 or so. It is leather and has a Welsh dragon on it, really beautiful.

I am using it to capture 7 to 10 line real-time poems, poems that unfold before me as I observe them.

I drive to the park and sit in the shade and write 10 lines about what actually is unfolding before my eyes. Later, I stare out the window at my house and write 7 lines about what is actually happening, detail by detail, with no philosophizing. Lastly, I take these two sittings of real-time writing and recopy them, reshuffling their lines into one poem. This has become my number one self prompt.

Gisèle Lewis

In a grocery-store parking lot, select a mundane or discarded object—an old hamburger wrapper, a rusty shopping cart, a stray cat. Personify it or embody its point of view to express the poignancy of everyday life. There are no restrictions except that the "item" not be a human.

Marjorie Maddox

Write a poem based on a billboard you've passed (perhaps very quickly) on the highway. What do you remember? Try to include a sense of speed and urgency.

Cameron Morse

Write a poem about yourself from the point of view of a family member. Stop. Then write a poem about yourself as a ghost from the point of view of the same family member.

Bruce Pemberton

"Charles Bukowski wrote over five thousand poems, most of which were composed and typed at his kitchen table late at night. Do you write at an unusual place? If so, describe it. If not, and you write at a traditional desk, describe THAT, and make a poem out of it either way."

Claudia M. Reder

Select a poet whose poems you love to read. Seek photos of their writing places: cabins, rooms, offices. Write down details of this space. Begin your poem by describing where they write. Now you enter the room and talk to the poet. Let the poet know how much their work has meant to you. You might begin a line, "In this poem I think you want to say..." You might include where you read a poem, imagine someone else finding the poem, and if you left the poem somewhere in the world, who do you hope would find it and read it and how would it change their life (or not).

Amy Small-McKinney

On one side of a blank page, list ten nouns. On the other side, ten verbs. Then circle only five nouns and five verbs. The key is to not think first, just circle. Write a poem, without censorship or consideration of meaning and theme, using these nouns and verbs. Surprise yourself.

Alison Stone

Take a well-known fairy tale or myth and examine it from a different angle. How might a minor character feel? What if the protagonist actually felt the opposite of how they're always portrayed? Is there a way that you connect emotionally to the story? This is a wonderful way to write about something deep and important to you without exposing personal details.

Barrett Warner

Find one thing in your life or story or poem you cannot live without. Maybe it's a guitar, or a hawk's feather. Now take it away. See what happens.

Contributor Notes

Katie Chicquette Adams is an educator and writer in Appleton, WI. A recent Pushcart nominee, her work has most recently appeared in *First Review East, Bramble, Wallopzine,* and *Portage Magazine.* She co-facilitates live storytelling with Storycatchers, and works as an English teacher for at-risk young adults at Appleton's public alternative high school, with hopes they will remake their own stories, and become friendly with at least one poem. She can be reached at k.chicquette.adams@gmail.com.

Diana Anhalt resided in Mexico City, MX for sixty years, but she and her husband moved to Atlanta, GA in order to be closer to family. (Although she left Mexico years ago, her poetry has refused to budge.) Her essays, newspaper articles, short stories and book reviews, in both English and Spanish, have been published in Mexico and the United States. She is the author of *A Gathering of Fugitives...* (Archer Books), and five chapbooks. Her most recent, *Walking Backward,* released this past summer, was the chapbook finalist for the Georgia Author of the Year Award.

Amy Baskin's work is currently featured in *Stone Gathering, The Midwest Quarterly,* and is forthcoming in *Friends Journal* and *Pilgrimage.* Her poems have been nominated for the Pushcart Prize and Best of the Net. She's an Oregon Literary Arts Fellow and an Oregon Poetry Association prize winner. When not writing, she matches international students at Lewis & Clark College with local residents to help them feel welcome and at home during their time in Oregon.

Lauren Camp is the author of five books, most recently *Took House* (Tupelo Press, 2020), which *Publishers Weekly* calls a "stirring, original collection." Her writing has appeared in numerous journals, including *The Los Angeles Review, Pleiades, Ecotone, Poet Lore,* and *DIAGRAM*. Honors include the Dorset Prize and finalist citations for the Arab American Book Award and the New Mexico-Arizona Book Award. Her work has been translated into Mandarin, Turkish, Spanish, and Arabic. www.laurencamp.com

Sarah Carleton writes poetry, edits fiction, tutors English, plays the banjo, and makes her husband laugh in Tampa, Florida. Her poems have appeared in numerous publications, including *Cider Press Review, Nimrod, Chattahoochee Review, Tar River Poetry, Crab Orchard Review* and *New Ohio Review.* Her first collection, *Notes from the Girl Cave,* (which includes the poem "Miami Airport Nocturne") was recently published by Kelsay Books.

Patrice Boyer Claeys is the author of two poetry collections: *The Machinery of Grace*

(2020) and *Lovely Daughter of the Shattering* (2019). Recent work appears or is forthcoming in *Zone 3, Glassworks Magazine, Inflectionist Review, Literary Mama, Neologism, Relief: Journal of Art and Faith, little somethings press, *82 Review* and *Aeolian Harp Anthology 5*. She was nominated for a Pushcart Prize and twice for Best of the Net. Patrice lives in Chicago and can be found online at www.patriceboyerclaeys.com.

Sara Comito is author of the new collection *Bury Me in the Sky* (Nixes Mate Books) and a poetry editor for *Bending Genres Journal*. Her work has recently been published in *Misfit Magazine, The Night Heron Barks, Ghost Parachute, Drunk Monkeys,* and *Pithead Chapel*. She works with her husband in their stone masonry business in Fort Myers, Florida, where they also run a tiny urban farm. Tweet her @Comito_writes.

Roger Craik has written four collections of poetry: *I Simply Stared* (2002), *Rhinoceros in Clumber Park,* (2003), *The Darkening Green* (2004), and *Down Stranger Roads* (2014), along with two chapbooks, *Those Years* (2007), (translated into Bulgarian in 2009), and *Of England Still* (2009). His poetry has appeared in several national poetry journals, such as *The Formalist, Fulcrum, The Literary Review, The Atlanta Review,* and *The London Magazine*.

English by birth and educated at the universities of Reading and Southampton, he has worked as a journalist, TV critic and chess columnist. Before coming to the USA in 1991, he worked in Turkish universities and was awarded a Beineke Fellowship to Yale in 1990. He is widely traveled, having visited North Yemen, Egypt, South Africa, Tibet, Nepal, Japan, Bulgaria (where he taught during spring 2007 on a Fulbright Scholarship), the United Arab Emirates, Austria, Croatia and Romania, (where from 2013-14 he was a Fulbright Scholar at the University of Oradea).

He is glad every day that he is living in the USA.

Darren C. Demaree is the author of fourteen poetry collections, most recently *Unfinished Murder Ballads*, (October 2020, Backlash Press). He is the recipient of a 2018 Ohio Arts Council Individual Excellence Award, the Louis Bogan Award from Trio House Press, and the Nancy Dew Taylor Award from *Emrys Journal*. He is the Managing Editor of the *Best of the Net Anthology* and *Ovenbird Poetry*. He is currently living in Columbus, Ohio with his wife and children.

Nepal-born **Anuja Ghimire** (Twitter @GhimireAnuja) lives near Dallas with her husband and two daughters. She writes poetry, flash fiction and creative nonfiction. She is the author of poetry chapbook *Kathmandu* (the Unsolicited Press). She's a *Best of the Net* and Pushcart nominee, a senior publisher in an online learning company, and a poetry reader for *Up the Staircase Quarterly*. Her work found home in *Glass: A journal of poetry, Orbis: London, EcoTheo Review, UCity Review,* and *Crack the Spine* among others.

Patrick Cabello Hansel is the author of the poetry collections *The Devouring Land* (Main Street Rag Publishing) and the forthcoming *Quitting Time* (Atmosphere Press). He has published poems and prose in over 65 journals, including *Crannog, Ilanot Review, Hawai'i Pacific Review, Ash & Bones, RiverSedge* and *Lunch Ticket,* and won awards from the Loft Literary Center and MN State Arts Board. His novella Searching was serialized in 33 issues of *The Alley News*. He is the editor of *The Phoenix of Phillips*, a literary journal by and for the most diverse community in Minneapolis.

Jennifer Jean's poetry collections include *The Fool* (Big Table) and *Object Lesson*—which is forthcoming from Lily Books in 2021. Her teaching resource *Object Lesson: A Guide to Writing Poetry* is also forthcoming in 2021. Her awards include: a Kenyon Review Writers Workshop Fellowship; a Disquiet Fellowship; and, an Ambassador for Peace Award for her activism in the arts. Jennifer's poems and co-translations have appeared in: *Poetry Magazine, Rattle Magazine, Waxwing Journal, Crab Creek Review, The Common,* and more. She is the founder of Free2Write Poetry Workshops for Trauma Survivors, an organizer for the Her Story Is collective, and the translations editor for *Talking Writing Magazine*. Jennifer lives in Massachusetts with her husband and children.

Allison Joseph lives, writes, and teaches in Carbondale, Illinois, where she is on the faculty at Southern Illinois University. Her most recent books are *Confessions of a Barefaced Woman* (Red Hen Press), *Smart Pretender* (Finishing Line) and *The Last Human Heart* (Diode Editions). Her next published collections will be *Lexicon,* also with Red Hen Press, and *Professional Happiness* (Backbone Press). She is the widow of Jon Tribble, the greatly missed poet, writer, and editor.

Jennifer Schomburg Kanke, originally from Columbus, Ohio, lives in Tallahassee, Florida, where she edits confidential documents for the government. Her work has appeared or is forthcoming in *New Ohio Review, Prairie Schooner,* and *Pleiades*. Her chapbook, *Fine, Considering*, about her experiences undergoing chemotherapy for ovarian cancer, is available from Rinky Dink Press. She serves as a reader for *Emrys*.

87

Lynne Knight is the author of six full-length poetry collections and six chapbooks. Her work has appeared many journals. Her awards and honors include publication in *Best American Poetry*, a PSA Lucille Medwick Memorial Award, a *RATTLE* Poetry Prize, and an NEA grant. She lives on Vancouver Island.

Rustin Larson's poetry has appeared in *The New Yorker, The Iowa Review,* and *North American Review.* He won 1st Editor's Prize from *Rhino* and was a prize winner in The National Poet Hunt and The Chester H. Jones Foundation contests. A graduate of the Vermont College MFA in Writing, Larson was an Iowa Poet at The Des Moines National Poetry Festival, and a featured poet at the Poetry at Round Top Festival. He is a poetry professor at Maharishi University, a writing instructor at Kirkwood Community College, and has also been a writing instructor at Indian Hills Community College. Among his published books are *Library Rain*, Conestoga Zen Press, 2019 which was named a February 2019 Exemplar by Grace Cavalieri and reviewed in *The Washington Independent Review of Books*; *Howling Enigma*, Conestoga Zen Press, 2018; *Pavement*, Blue Light Press, 2017; *The Philosopher Savant*, Glass Lyre Press, 2015; *Bum Cantos, Winter Jazz, & The Collected Discography of Morning*, Blue Light Press, 2013; *The Wine-Dark House*, Blue Light Press, 2009; and *Crazy Star*, Loess Hills Books, 2005. His honors and awards also include Pushcart Prize Nominee (seven times, 1988-2010); featured writer, DMACC Celebration of the Literary Arts, 2007, 2008; and finalist, New England Review Narrative Poetry Competition, 1985.

Gisèle Lewis is a native Bostonian transplanted to sweltering Florida. She spends her days parenting and her nights writing. Her secondary passions include volunteering for a refugee women's support nonprofit, synchronized swimming, and teaching her daughters to curse in French. Her short fiction has been published in the *Baltimore Review* and the *Havik!* 2018 Anthology.

Winner of *America Magazine's* 2019 Foley Poetry Prize and Professor of English and Creative Writing at Lock Haven University, **Marjorie Maddox** has published 11 collections of poetry—including *Transplant, Transport, Transubstantiation* (Yellowglen Prize); *True, False, None of the Above* (Illumination Book Award Medalist); *Local News from Someplace Else; Perpendicular As I*(Sandstone Book Award)—the short story collection *What She Was Saying* (Fomite); children's books; *Common Wealth: Contemporary Poets on Pennsylvania* (co-editor); *Presence* (assistant editor); and 600+ stories, essays, and poems in journals and anthologies. Her book *Begin with a Question* is forthcoming from Paraclete Press Fall 2021. www.marjoriemaddox.com

Charissa Menefee co-directs the MFA Program in Creative Writing & Environment at Iowa State University. Her poetry can be found in her book, *When I Stopped Counting*, as well as literary journals, anthologies, and Telepoem Booths. She was recently awarded a 2020/2021 EST/Sloan Project commission for a new play, and is the founder and artistic director of The EcoTheatre Lab. (www.charissamenefee.com)

Cameron Morse lives with his wife Lili and two children in Independence, Missouri. His first collection, *Fall Risk*, won Glass Lyre Press's 2018 Best Book Award. His latest is Baldy (Spartan Press, 2020). He holds and MFA from the University of Kansas City—Missouri and serves as a poetry editor at *Harbor Review* and the poetry editor at Harbor Editions.

Bruce Pemberton is a retired high school teacher, coach, and Gulf War veteran. His most recent work has appeared in *American Life In Poetry, Third Wednesday, Sky Island Journal, iTeach Literary Magazine,* and the anthologies, *In Tahoma's Shadow, Spokane Writes,* and *The Poet.* He lives on the Palouse, in rural, eastern Washington state.

Claudia M. Reder is the author of *How to Disappear,* a poetic memoir, (Blue Light Press, 2019). *Uncertain Earth* (Finishing Line Press), and *My Father & Miro* (Bright Hill Press). She was awarded the Charlotte Newberger Poetry Prize from *Lilith Magazine,* and two literary fellowships from the Pennsylvania Arts Council. She teaches at California State University at Channel Islands. For many years she has been a poet/storyteller in the Schools.

Amy Small-McKinney's poems have been published in numerous journals, for example, *Connotation Press, Construction, American Poetry Review, The Indianapolis Review, Tiferet, Anomaly, Ilanot Review,* and *Pedestal Magazine.* She has also been a guest editor for *Pedestal Magazine.* Her poem "Birthplace" received Special Merits recognition by *The Comstock Review* for their 2019 Muriel Craft Bailey Poetry Contest. Her second full-length book of poems, *Walking Toward Cranes,* won the Kithara Book Prize 2016 (Glass Lyre Press). Her poems have also been translated into Romanian and Korean. Her reviews of poetry books have been published in several journals, for example, Prairie Schooner. Small-McKinney has an MS in Clinical Neuropsychology from Drexel University and an MFA in Poetry from Drew University.

Alison Stone has published six full-length collections, *Caught in the Myth* (NYQ Books, 2019), *Dazzle* (Jacar Press, 2017), *Masterplan,* a book of collaborative poems with Eric Greinke (Presa Press, 2018), *Ordinary Magic,* (NYQ Books, 2016), *Dangerous Enough*

(Presa Press 2014), and *They Sing at Midnight*, which won the 2003 Many Mountains Moving Poetry Award; as well as three chapbooks. Her poems have appeared in *The Paris Review, Poetry, Ploughshares, Barrow Street, Poet Lore,* and many other journals and anthologies. She has been awarded *Poetry's* Frederick Bock Prize and *New York Quarterly's* Madeline Sadin Award. She was Writer in Residence at LitSpace St. Pete. She is also a painter and the creator of The Stone Tarot. A licensed psychotherapist, she has private practices in NYC and Nyack. www.stonepoetry.org www.stonetarot.com. YouTube – Alison Stone Poetry.

Barrett Warner is the author of *Why Is It So Hard to Kill You?* (Somondoco, 2016) and *My Friend Ken Harvey* (Publishing Genius, 2014). He keeps a shy beat, rubbing horses in training and foaling mares, and his poems appear recently in *Beloit Poetry Journal, Rabbit Catastrophe Review, Anti-Heroin Chic, Taco Bell Quarterly,* and *Carolina Quarterly*. He was awarded a Maryland individual artist award for his farm essays, as well as the :Liam Rector poetry prize, and the Salamander fiction prize. He also corners the oval as editor of *Free State Review*.

Glass Lyre Press

exceptional works to replenish the spirit

Glass Lyre Press is an independent literary publisher interested in technically accomplished, stylistically distinct, and original work. Glass Lyre seeks diverse writers that possess a dynamic aesthetic and an ability to emotionally and intellectually engage a wide audience of readers.

Glass Lyre's vision is to connect the world through language and art. We hope to expand the scope of poetry and short fiction for the general reader through exceptionally well-written books, which evoke emotion, provide insight, and resonate with the human spirit.

Poetry Collections
Poetry Chapbooks
Select Short & Flash Fiction
Anthologies

www.GlassLyrePress.com

www.ingramcontent.com/pod-product-compliance
Lightning Source LLC
LaVergne TN
LVHW040108080526
838202LV00045B/3830